THINK OUT YOUR DESTINY
"SUCCESS BEGINS IN THE FORM OF A THOUGHT"

Think Out Your Destiny

"Obtain Your Success"

By

Kayode Eniraiyetan

JESUS FRIENDS MINISTRY PUBLISHING

THINK OUT YOUR DESTINY
"SUCCESS BEGINS IN THE FORM OF A THOUGHT"

KAYODE ENIRAIYETAN

JESUS' FRIENDS MINISTRY

53, Northfleet House,

Tabard Garden Estate,

London. SE1 1YX.

Tel. & Fax: 02036384720.

Mob.07427942000, 07951775255.

e-mail: jesusfriends28@yahoo.com

Website: www.jesusfriendsministry.com

Text C Kayode Eniraiyetan 2018

ISBN: 978-0-9563295-6-1

Books by same author –1. **Affliction- Fruit of Sin. 2. The Redeemed Man. 3.King David's Twelve Steps To Success. 4. 7 Walls Surrounding A Born Again Christian. 5. Born Poor: Die Rich.**

Direct copyright enquires to; **Jesus' Friends Ministry.**

THINK OUT YOUR DESTINY

Unless otherwise stated, all scripture quotations are taken from;

The Holy Bible – King James Version, Dake's Annotated Reference Bible,

Bible Basics (Discovering Truth Series),

The Oxford Companion to the Bible – Mtzger&Coogan.

All rights reserved. No part of this publication may be reproduced, stored in a retrieval system, or transmitted in any form, or by any means, electronic, mechanical, photocopying, recording or otherwise without the prior written permission of the publisher, or except in the case of brief quotations embodied in critical reviews and certain other non-commercial uses permitted by copyright law.

Copyright © 2018   Kayode Eniraiyetan

All rights reserved.

ISBN: 978-0-9563295-6-1

DEDICATION

Dedicated to my family, friends and acquaintances who desire to consecrate themselves as;
"Highest Good Of Being For All".

CONTENTS

	Acknowledgments	i
1	Thought Defined.	1
2	Destiny.	7
3	Man's Destiny.	13
4	Think Out Your Destiny.	19
5	Our Lives Are What Our Thoughts Make Of Them.	25
6	The Act Of Thinking.	29
7	Mastermind Principle.	33
8	Infinite Intelligence.	39
9	Circles Of Life.	49
10	The World At Large.	53
11	More World At Large.	61
12	Ages And World Dispensations.	73
13	Conclusion.	97

PREFACE.

In a mental hospital, the decision to admit a new intake is determined this way;

Bathtub is filled with water and then the intake is given a teaspoon, a glass and a bucket. He or she will then be asked to empty the bathtub using one of the items given.

A normal person would pull the drain plug. If you choose the bucket, you are not using your brain. You are not thinking.

When you fail to think, you limit yourself to superficial conditions and make yourself a beast of burden for those who think.

Unless you are willing to think, you shall have to work, and the less you think, the more you shall have to work and the less you shall get for your work.

Everybody created had been endowed with the talent and skill needed for his/her survival and to fulfill the purpose of his/her life.

You therefore offends humanity if you are ordinary.

Kayode Eniraiyetan.

ACKNOWLEDGEMENT

Acknowledgement solely to GOD the FATHER, GOD the SON and GOD the HOLY GHOST who are the providers of all the ingredients for this book.

THINK OUT YOUR DESTINY
"SUCCESS BEGINS IN THE FORM OF A THOUGHT"

CHAPTER ONE

THOUGHT DEFINED.

To think is the process of considering or reasoning about something. To have or formulate in the mind. To direct one's mind towards someone or something; use of one's mind actively to form connected ideas. To conceive of in the mind.
To think means to have Clear, Decisive, Calm, Deliberate, Sustained thought with a definite end in view. Thinking is the act of using one's mind to produce thoughts.

The mind is the factory where our thoughts are manufactured. This is then followed by our action and deeds. The ability of the individual to think is his ability to act. The dominating thought which a man permits to occupy his mind determines what he is. For every man is the reflection of the thought he has entertained during his lifetime. This is stamped on his face, his form, his character and his environment.

An idea is a thought **conceived in the mind and this rational form of the thought is the root of form, in the sense that this form of thought is the initial formal expression that acting upon substance causes it to form.**

Mind is then the source of all things, in the sense that the activity of mind is the initial cause of all things coming into being. It is the essence of a thing that constitutes its being and the activity of mind is the cause by which the essence takes form.

THOUGHT; (The Secret of All Attainment)
"**Thinking is the act of using one's mind to produce thoughts**"

Thinking is the act of using one's mind to produce thoughts. Thoughts refers to ideas or arrangement of ideas that are the result of the process of thinking. Or processes thinking is an activity considered essential to humanity, there is no consensus as to how we define or understand it.

Because thought underlies many human actions and interactions, understanding its physical and metaphysical origins, process and effects has been a longstanding goal of many academic disciplines.

Thinking allows humans to make sense of, interpret, or model the world they experience, and to make predictions about that world. It is therefore helpful to an organism with needs, objectives and desires as it makes plans or otherwise attempts to accomplish those goals.

What relationship exists between mind or mental process and bodily states or processes? What is the nature of the mind and mental states and how or if minds are affected by or can affect the body?

Human perpetual experiences depend on stimuli which arrive at one's various sensory organs from the external world and these stimuli cause changes in one's mental state, ultimately causing one to fell a sensation, which may be pleasant or unpleasant. Someone's desire for clothing, for example, will tend to cause that person to move his or her body in a specific manner and in a specific direction to obtain what he or she wants. How then is it possible for conscious experience to arise out of a lump of gray matter endowed with nothing but electrochemical properties.

A related problem is to explain how someone's proportional attitude like beliefs and desire can cause that individual's neurons to fire and his muscles to contract in exactly the correct manner.

This reflects a classical functional description of how we work as cognitive thinking systems. To separate the mind and analyze it alone will be misguided, instead we should see that the mind, actions of an embodied agent and the environment it perceives and envisions are all parts of a whole which determines each other. Functional analysis of the mind alone will leave us with the mind-body problem which cannot be solved.

The most powerful forces of Nature are the invisible forces, and the most powerful forces of man are his invisible forces – his Spiritual Force – and the only way in which the Spiritual Force can manifest is through the process of thinking.

Thinking is the only activity which the Spirit possesses and thought is the only product of thinking.

Addition and Subtraction are Spiritual transactions, Reasoning is a Spiritual process, Ideas are Spiritual

Conceptions, Questions are Spiritual searchlights and logic, Argument and Philosophy are Spiritual machineries.

Every thought brings into action certain physical tissue on part of the brain, nerve or muscle. This produces an actual physical change in the construction of the tissue; therefore it is only necessary to have a certain number of thoughts on a given subject in order to bring about a complete change in the physical organization of a man.

This is the process by which failure is changed to success; Thought of courage, power, inspiration, harmony are substituted for thoughts of failure, despair, lack, limitation and discord. As these thoughts take root, the physical tissue is changed and the individual sees life in a new light, old things have actually passed away, all things have become new. He is born again, this time born of the Spirit; life has a new meaning for him; he is reconstructed and is filled with joy, confidence, hope and energy. He sees opportunities for success to which he was heretofore blind.

He recognizes possibilities which before had no meaning for him. The thoughts of success with which he has been impregnated are radiated to those around him, and they in turn help him onward and upward. He attracts to himself new and successful associates and this in turn changes his environment; so that by this simple exercise of thought, a man changes not only himself but his environment, circumstances and conditions.

DESIRE BACKED BY FAITH KNOWS NO

THINK OUT YOUR DESTINY

SUCH WORD AS IMPOSSIBLE.
It all starts with the desire to succeed and the believe that you will succeed.

EVERY FAILURE BRINGS WITH IT THE SEED OF AN EQUIVALENT SUCCESS.
You only need to find the seed.

THOUGHT; (The Secret of All Attainment)

"SUCCESS BEGINS IN THE FORM OF A THOUGHT"

CHAPTER TWO

DESTINY.

Oxford Dictionary defines destiny as the events that will necessarily happen to a particular person or thing in the future. It is the hidden power believed to control future events. It is fate of a person or a thing.

The destiny is not determined by the recipient or the operator but by our maker. None the less it is the responsibility of the owner of the destiny to discover his or her destiny and the earlier the better for the person.

As there is destiny for individuals, so also there is destiny for the world as a whole. And like each one of us, the world's destiny had been determined by God, Creator of heaven and the earth.

Destiny is what keeps everything moving forward. Destiny is what generates the motivation to create, to establish, to explore and to fulfil.

There is a destiny for you, and there is a destiny for the world. Your destiny here is to find your purpose and to find your allies, those unique individuals who are here to help you fulfil that purpose.

WORLD'S DESTINY

God has a plan; which is the world's destiny.
The destiny of the world is Dispensational Plan of God for the Universe from Eternal Past through Eternal Future.

It is the drafting of God's plan and it's manifestation from eternal past all through the two creations, dispensation of Angels, dispensation of Man to New Heavens and the New Earth.
This is The Kingdom of God Universal – God the Supreme Moral Governor of the Universe, and everything in harmony with Him. God All-in-All.

God's plan for the world is to become New Heavens and New Earth when the earth will be in perfect state eternally with God all-in-all again. That was the situation before the rebellion in the universe headed by Lucifer and the Fall by Adam.
God in the Eternal past drafted His plan and established the Creation of the Heavens, including the sun, moon and the stars. Spirit world was created and followed by the creation of earth made perfect the first time.

The world (kosmos) social order that then was created. Here Lucifer reigned over the world that then was. The length of his rule is not known.

Other thrones, dominions, principalities and powers were created and placed over other parts of the universe.

The kingdom of God Universal where God the Supreme Moral Governor of the Universe established and everything in harmony with Him.

The length of time of rule of the Universal Harmonious Kingdom before Lucifer's rebellion is not known.

Lucifer, the original ruler of the planet earth, conceived an idea that he can obtain cooperation of other angelic beings, dethrone God and become the exalted supreme ruler universe himself.

He carried his plan, falls through pride and slanders the Almighty, causing his own subjects and over one third of God's angels to rebel against God. This is the first sinful career of the earth. The length of the uprising is unknown.

Lucifer openly breaks relation with God and His government, leading his rebels from the appointed place of mobilization on earth into heaven in his attempt to dethrone God. He was met with Michael and the faithful Angels and is defeated, being cast as lighting back to the earth.

God destroyed Lucifer's kingdom on earth completely, and cursed the earth by destroying every birds, animals, fishes, cities, inhabitants and all vegetation. God then turned the earth upside down, and by means of a great flood makes it empty and a waste. Length of the pre-Adamite flood on earth is unknown.

What followed next was the beginning of the heavens and earth which are now with its recreation in 6 literal 24-hour days starting from Genesis 1-3.

The Spirit of God moves upon the flooded earth in the darkness covering the waters. Light is restored; earth is brought to a second habitable state. New land animals, fish, fowls and vegetation are created.

Adam is made the new ruler of the earth in Lucifer's place.

The earth is made perfect the second time, all things in the Universe are again in harmony with God as before Lucifer and his spirit rebelled who are still at large in the heavenliest. They are being permitted to remain free to further God's plan by testing man in the probationary periods of the human race.

Thus, the restored earth entered its first Probationary Period. This is called "Dispensation of Innocence". Length of this period is very short – starts with creation of Adam and ends at the Fall of Man. 6 days.

Lucifer (now the devil and adversary of God and man, called Satan), enters the restored earth, tempts man and caused his fall, thus regaining dominion of the earth and all things therein. Rebellion is begun on the earth again by its second ruler, Adam.

Man is judged, the earth is cursed again and it enters its second sinful career with all creatures being brought under bondage of sin and corruption.

Beginning from the Fall of man, the heaven and the earth which are now, await the time of the second renovation and this will usher in the third perfect state called "The New Heaven and the New Earth".

This second renovation shall be the second resurrection and final judgment at the end of the Millennium. It shall be the end of Earth's second sinful career and renovation of the immediate heavens and the earth by fire and removal of all the curses and their effects together with confinement of all spirits and human rebels of all ages in the lake of fire forever.

The new Heaven and the New Earth, now perfect the third time, shall continue in eternal perfect state with God all-in-all as before rebellion in the Universe headed by Lucifer and Adam.

This is the world's destiny and God's plan. It cannot change but rather everything must occur in harmony and in conformity with the plan of God.

Human being are individually created to play his or her parts individually towards the manifestation and for the establishment of this God's plan and the world's destiny.

This is where it is heading. It is going in this direction no matter what human society is doing. It must go in this direction. This represents the next stage of life in the world. It is inevitable and unalterable. The two rebellions cannot change God's plan for the world.

"THE GREATEST ACHIEVEMENT WAS AT FIRST, AND FOR A TIME, BUT A THOUGHT".

CHAPTER THREE

MAN'S DESTINY

Man is created to carry out God's plan for the world to its manifestation and establishment.

A man's destiny is not determined by him but by God, his creator. Nonetheless, it is for him to discover his destiny and the earlier he does so, the better for him.

God created man to see to the manifestation of His plan for the world at large. Each individual created has a part to play in the realization of the world's destiny. That we are part of the plan of God to fulfill world's destiny does not make Him to enforce it on us to follow His own plan for us. He allows us to choose our paths.

He gave us the choice to choose between the path of Righteousness and the path of Evil. Whatever choice we choose has its consequence, hence we are given the right to make our choice, but we are not given the choice of the consequence of whatever path we choose to follow.

Whatever we sow: that we shall reap.

It is God's ultimate plan to rid the universe of all rebellions so that all free moral agents will be willingly and eternally subject to God, To Christ and

To the Holy Ghost as originally planned with God all-in-all forever. This plan can never change or be altered.

When God created man, he was made in God's image and likeness. He was formed from the dust of the earth and God, "The Infinite" breathed into him "The Finite".

This Divine Breath of God in man became the benignant force which decrees primal creation. It comes from God and direct into every created being and became Divine Heredity. It originates life and flows through each individual created and comprise its consciousness.

The same spirit that sleeps in the mineral breathes in the vegetable, moves in the animal and reaches its highest development in MAN.

It gives man the power to THINK and exercise his dominion over what his creator bestowed on him.

Thus man is deemed to be fulfilling his destiny and performing the purpose of his creation when he THINKS and ACTS in harmony with God's plan for his life using the talents and skills his creator provided for him.

Man's objective and purpose must be constructive and must be in harmony with the creative principle of his CREATOR. This is when, and the only way, he is living his life in accordance with the purpose of his creation.

God acts through the individual and the individual can achieve nothing except allowed by his creator.

A PART MUST BE THE SAME IN KIND AND QUALITY AS THE WHOLE. The only difference is one of degree. For God is the WHOLE and individual is the part. THEY ARE ONE.

The "I" of you is not the physical body; that is simply an instrument which the "I" uses to carry out its purpose. The "I" cannot be the mind, for the mind is simply another instrument which the "I" uses with which to think, reason and plan.

The "I" must be something which controls and directs both the body and the mind, something which determines what they should do and how they should act.

When a man say "I think" the "I" tells his mind what it shall think; when the man say "I go" the "I" tells the physical body where it shall go. The real nature of this "I" is spiritual. It is the source of the real power which the man derives from the "Breath of Life" breathed into him by God when he was created and which had become his Divine Heredity.

In the route of our ancestry, specific lines were travelled and specific character established. We lose neither the one nor the other, for both lines and character are projected from generation to generation.

The lines, though invisible, are never broken, nor are they ever abruptly changed to other type of expressions. Neither are the characteristic ever lost, though they continue to project from generation to generation down through the ages.

It is an established fact that man is 10% Conscious and 90% Subconscious. The Subconscious part of him is his "World Within" and this is controlled by the "I" and that this "I" is a part or one with the Infinite "I" which is the Universal Energy, the

Universal Spirit which we call GOD. The Omnipotent, Omniscience, Omnipresent. God All-in-All.

Each individual created is a part of the "Whole" where the "Whole" is the CREATOR.

A part must be the same in kind and quality as the whole; the only difference there can possibly be is in degree.

The "I", the Spirit which thinks is an integral part of the great whole, same in substance, in quality, in kind.

The Creator will not create nothing different from Himself, "The Father and I are one". A drop of water from the ocean is the same in kind and quality as the ocean; the difference is in degree. Same Quality, Different Quantity.

Your destiny, then, is upon you. It is not in the distant future where you do not have to think about it. It is happening right now. You are in it. Become a contributor to it. Prepare. Gain access to Knowledge, the Knowing Mind within you, and the greater purpose which has brought you here, for this will teach you how to prepare and this will enable to prepare . This will show you who you need to be with and where you need to be in life.

The greatness of your mission must become known to you because the world needs its expression and demonstration. The greatness of your contribution is needed because the needs of humanity will only grow and become more severe.

Your destiny is presented here in order to enable you to open your eyes. It is presented here more as a gift than as a warning. You know it is coming. And you now have the opportunity to prepare. And you know that you need to prepare. The preparation for the New World is being given to you in New World Way of Knowledge. You have it before you at this moment. Do not judge it from your past references, but open yourself to it as a preparation for the future and as a means of gaining access to what you know and what you can do now.

KAYODE ENIRAIYETAN

"Thought concentrated on a definite purpose becomes Power"

CHAPTER FOUR

THINK OUT YOUR DESTINY
(Thought concentrated on a definite purpose becomes Power)

To think your destiny out is to consider or reason out your destiny, to discover your destiny, to have or conceive in mind what your destiny is. To meditate on your destiny having a clear, decisive, calm and sustainable thought on why you are created and your purpose in life.

Your destiny is not determined by you, but it has to be discovered by you. The beginning of your discovery is your thought of it leading you to your realization and achievement.

Your destiny is peculiar and unique to you the way your fingerprint is unique to you. NO TWO DESTINIES ARE THE SAME. It is not the same with your ancestors neither is it the same with your parent's destiny.

You are created for a time like this, for the purpose like this and for the needs of the world like this.

When you were born, you came to the world with the talent and the skill needed by you to fulfill your destiny on earth.

Your circumstances, your condition, the experience you encounter in life are not there by accident, rather they were there to help you find out your purpose. To call your destiny out of you. You must go into the world and have it brought out of you. The world you are in is for your destiny to be initiated, fostered and realized, hence seeking a retreat or escape will be counter-productive.

The very tribulations and adversities you encounter in the world that you find so unpleasant and difficult are the very catalyst to bring out of you greatness in you that you have come to give to the world. The service you have come to render.

This is why it is important for you to discover in time, the reason for your existence. The earlier you discover your destiny, the better for you since you stand the chance to make correction and retreat if you miss your way or derail along the way.

Your destiny is your route which you have to follow in your journey of life. Finding the way early in your life is important. It is the destination you must reach and finding the right means of getting there in time is a privilege not given to many. A gift from God.

When taking your bus to your place of work in a typical working day, you need the right bus. You may never get to your destination if you end up with the wrong bus or be late if you get there at all or end up in a wrong destination, just for entering the wrong bus.

A person that realize his mistake in time when in the wrong bus needs to make immediate correction if he is to have a success journey. LIFE IS A JOURNEY.

Every thought creates an impression on the brain, these impressions create mental tendencies and these tendencies create character, ability and purpose.

The combined action of character, ability and purpose determine the experience with which we shall meet in life.

These experiences come to us through the Law of Attraction. Through the action of this law we meet in the world without the experiences which correspond to our world within.

The predominant thought or the mental attitude is the magnet, and the law is that "like attracts like". Consequently, the mental attitude will invariably attract such conditions as correspond to its nature.

This mental attitude is our personality and is composed of the thoughts which we have been creating in our mind; therefore, if we wish a change in conditions , all that is necessary is to change our thoughts.

This will in turn change our mental attitude, which will in turn change our personality, which will in turn change the persons, things and conditions or the experiences with which we meet in life.

THE PYRAMID WITH FOUR SIDES.

Life is a journey where the destination is the peak of a pyramid with four sides. You are not a success until you are at the peak of the pyramid.

Each side has different features and hence different means of getting to the top of the pyramid. The four sides represent four different journey of mankind on his road to success.

Some come to the world on the side with easy

access to the peak of the pyramid. To such, there is a natural lift which they only need to press a button and they are lifted up to the peak of the pyramid of life. These are those born with the proverbial "Silver Spoon" in their mouth.

Another side is equipped with natural steps like a ladder. Each steps takes those on this side nearer to the peak of the pyramid. There are lessons to be learnt at each stage and step with its associated ups and downs. Naturally each step must be taken one at a time, and if you are in harmony with natural order of things, you will attain success, power and wealth with very little conscious efforts.

Some are born to the side whose sloppy feature makes it look like a cliff. Here, you need a rope to get to get to the top. But let me assure you, there is always an invisible rope for those that God destined to get to the top. We call it a miracle when it appears.

The fourth side is very slippery. This side is covered with snow that had turned to ice. Unless you follow a mentor who leads and create steps on the ice along the way, for you to step on, getting to the top will be a mirage.

There are some common features to all travelers on this journey of life and our road to success. No one is born blank. We all come to this world equipped with tools needed for each to build his or her Temple of Success.

Different as they are, these are talents and skills given to us by our creator. We do not determine them, but we are to discover them. The earlier we discover them, the easier for us to fulfill our purpose in life and the earlier we construct our Temple of

Success.

When we are born into this world, we were endowed with certain inborn traits, the result of millions of years of evolutionary changes and heredity of thousands ancestors.

Added to these inborn traits we acquire other qualities according to the nature of our environments and the teaching we received during our early childhood.

We are therefore the sum total of that which was born in us and that which we have picked up from our experiences, what we have thought and what we have been taught since birth.

Application of all the above in us, together with our desire to be successful is all what we need to reach the top, the peak of our pyramid irrespective of which side we find ourselves, irrespective of how, where and when we are born, all things being equal.

WE ARE THE ARCHITECT OF OUR TEMPLE OF SUCCESS.

The tools to construct this temple are our thoughts and our actions. How we think and what we do.

DESIRE BACKED BY FAITH KNOWS NO SUCH WORD AS IMPOSSIBLE.

CHAPTER FIVE

OUR LIFES ARE WHAT OUR THOUGHTS MAKE OF THEM.

If we think happy thoughts, we will be happy,
If we think miserable thoughts, we will be miserable,
If we think fear thoughts, we will be fearful,
If we think sickly thoughts, we will probably be ill,
If we think failure, we will certainly fail,
If we wallow in self-pity, everyone will want to shun us and avoid us,
YOU ARE NOT WHAT YOU THINK YOU ARE, BUT WHAT YOU THINK, YOU ARE.

Our thoughts make us what we are; the only problem we have to deal with is choosing the right thoughts.

The first form which thought will find is language or words. This shows how important WORDS are. They are the first manifestation of thought – the vessels in which thought is carried.

They take hold of the ether and by setting it in motion reproduce the thought to others in the form of sound.

Thought may lead to action of any kind, but whatever the action, it is simply the thought attempting to express itself in visible form.

It is evident, therefore, that if we wish desirable

conditions, we must entertain only desirable thoughts.

Thought is the only reality, conditions are but the outward manifestations. As the thought changes, all outward or material conditions must change in order to be in harmony with their creator, which is thought.

The important thing is that the thought must be CLEAR CUT, STEADY, FIXED, DEFINITE and UNCHANGEABLE; otherwise, you will be taking one step forward and two steps backward. You cannot spend twenty or thirty years of your life building negative conditions as the result of negative thoughts and then expect to see them all melt away as the result of fifteen or twenty minutes of right thinking.

WRONG THINKING BRINGS FAILURE; SUCCESS IS EVIDENCE OF CORRECT THINKING. Purify the source and you have a flow of clear river.

Human consciousness consists only in the ability of man to think, Mind in itself is believed to be a subtle form of static energy from which arises activities called THOUGHT which is the dynamic phase of the mind.

Mind is static energy, thought is dynamic energy – the two phases of the same thing.

Thought is therefore the vibrating force formed by converting static mind into dynamic mind.

The mind normally takes on the nature of the influences which dominate it. That is why it is essential for us to encourage the positive emotions as dominating forces of our mind and discourage and eliminate any negative emotions.

THINK OUT YOUR DESTINY

Thought is a product of Mind and Mind is creative in nature. Thought contains a vital principle because it is the creative principle of the Universe and by its nature will combine with other similar thoughts.

As the one purpose of life is growth, all principles underlying existence must contribute to give it effect. Thought therefore takes form, and the law of growth eventually brings it into manifestation.

You may freely choose what you think, but the result of your thought is governed by an immutable law.

Any line of thought you persisted in cannot fail to produce its result in the character, health and circumstances of the individual. Methods whereby we can substitute habits of constructive thinking for those which we have found to produce only undesirable effects are therefore of primary important.

If your thought has been critical or destructive, and has resulted in any condition of discord or unharmonious in your environment, it may be necessary for you to cultivate a mental attitude which will be conductive to constructive thought.

Thought is a spiritual activity and is therefore creative, but make no mistake, thought will create nothing unless it is conspicuously, systematically and constructively directed. Herein is the difference between idle thinking, which is simply a dissipation of effort and constructive thinking, which means practically unlimited achievement.

We have found that everything we get comes to us by the Law of Attraction. A happy thought cannot exist in an unhappy consciousness, therefore the conscious must change, and, as the consciousness changes, all conditions necessary to meet the changed consciousness must gradually change in other to meet the requirement of the new situation.

Thought brings initiative; INITIATIVE backed by FAITH and the ZEAL to win is guaranteed SUCCESS.

CHAPTER SIX

THE ACT OF THINKING.

The only thing that differentiates a man from an animal is man's ability to THINK.

Mind is the workshop of THOUGHT. Man's thought is being influenced by many factors; Heredity, Environments, Information, |Knowledge and Experience.

THE DOMINATING THOUGHT OF A MAN DETERMINES WHAT BECOMES OF HIM.

Man has the freedom to choose how he thinks and his choice determines his end result. All thoughts originate from one source, The MIND. Though they originate from one source, their end results are diverse.

We act the way we think, hence;

He who thinks abnormal and acts same is termed MAD.

He who thinks low, stupid and idiotic is termed IMBECILE.

He who thinks and acts rashly, unwisely, who is artless, guileless and inconsiderate is SIMPLE. (In fact, a whole book of the Scripture is devoted for such)

He who thinks and acts selfish and infringe on the rights of others is termed WICKED and EVIL.

He who thinks and acts considerate,

constructively and go about doing good is termed GOOD.

He who thinks and acts supernaturally, above normal is termed A GENIUS. They tab and make use of their subconscious more than others.

A MADMAN ALSO THINKS; ONLY HE THINKS ABNORMALLY.

The source of our power is in our THOUGHT, and when we think Accurately and Constructively and for the good of all, we become SUPERMAN.

Man can create nothing which he does not first conceive in the form of an impulse of thought. And man's thought impulse begins immediately to translate themselves into their physical equivalent, whether those thoughts are voluntary or involuntary.

Thought impulses which are picked up through the ether, by mere chance may determines one's financial, business, professional or social destiny just as surely as do the thought impulse which one creates by intent or design.

This is laying the foundation for the presentation of a fact of great importance to the person who does not understand why some people appear to be lucky while others of equal or greater ability, training, experience, and brain capacity seem destiny to ride with misfortune.

This fact may be explained by the statement that every human being has the ability to completely control his own mind, and with this control, obviously, every person may open his mind to the tramp through impulses which are being released by other brains or close the doors tightly and admit only thought impulses of his own choice. Nature has endowed man with absolute control over but one thing and that is THOUGHT.

This fact, coupled with the additional fact that everything which man creates, begins in the form of a thought, leads one very near to the principle by which fear may be mastered.

A PART MUST BE THE SAME IN KIND AND QUALITY AS THE WHOLE.

CHAPTER SEVEN

MASTER MIND PRINCIPLE

The human mind is a form of energy, a part of it being spiritual in nature. When the mind of two people are coordinated in a SPIRIT of HAMONY, the spiritual units of energy of each mind form an affinity, which constitutes the psychic phase of the Master Mind.

This psychic phase of the Master Mind principle is much more abstract, much more difficult to comprehend because it has reference to the spiritual forces with which the human race, as a whole, is not well acquainted. **No two minds ever come together without, thereby, creating a third, invincible, intangible force which may be likened to a third mind.**
There are only two known elements in the whole inverse; ENERGY and MATTER. Matter can be broken down into units of Molecules, Atoms and Electrons. These may be isolated, separated and analyzed. Likewise, there are units of energy.

Energy is nature's universal set of building blocks, out of which she constructs every material thing in the universe, including man, and every form of animal and vegetable life.

Through a process which only Nature completely understands, she translates energy into matter.

Nature's building blocks are available to man, in the energy involved in THINKING.

Man's brain may be compared to an electric battery. It absorbs energy from the ether, which permeates every atom of matter and fills the entire universe.

It is a well-known fact that an individual battery will provide energy in proportion to the number and capacity of the cells it contains.

The brain functions in a similar fashion. This accounts for why some brains are more efficient than others. Thus a group of brains coordinated in a spirit of harmony, will provide more thought energy than a single brain, just as a group of electronic batteries will provide more energy than a single battery.

Through this it becomes obvious that the Master Mind principle holds the secret of the Power wielded by men who surround themselves with other men of brains.

Interestingly, whenever a group of individual brains are coordinated and function in Harmony, the increased energy created through that alliance becomes available to every individual brain in the group. It does not eradicate the individual brains but rather it compliments and supports.

Men take on the nature and the habits and the power of thought of those with whom they associate in a spirit of sympathy and harmony.

Thus man can whip poverty, illiteracy ignorance by allying with great minds, whose vibration is absorbed in his own mind. Added to his own brain power will be the sum and substance of the intelligence, experience, knowledge and spiritual forces of the great minds so allied. THIS IS MASTER MIND PRINCIPLE.

Our daily associates constitute one of the most important parts of our environment and may work for our progress or our retrogression according to the nature of such associates.

Our association must therefore be those who are in sympathy with our main goals, whose mental attitude inspire us with enthusiasm, self-confidence, determination and ambition.

Any form of group ort, where two or more people form a cooperative alliance for the purpose of accomplishing a goal, becomes more powerful than mere individual effort.

Plain cooperative effort produces power; there can be no doubt about this, but cooperative effort that is based upon complete harmony of purpose develops superpower.

Men who have been successful have been known as able organizers in that they possessed the ability to enlist the cooperative efforts of other men who supplied talent and ability which they themselves did not possess.

The organization must consist of individuals each of whom supplies some specialized talent which the other members of the organization do not possess.

Success cannot be attained single-handedly or independently. Fortunes that are acquired through cooperative effort inflict no scar upon the hearts of their owners, but not so for fortunes that are acquired through conflict and competitive methods that border on extortion.

MASTERS OF FATE; THE CAPTAIN OF SOULS.

We have the power to control our thoughts; hence we are the Masters of our fate, the Captains of our souls.

The ether in which this our earth floats and in which we move and have our being is a form of energy moving at an inconceivable high rate of vibration. This ether is filled with a form of Universal Power which adapts itself to the nature of the thoughts we hold in our minds; and influences us, in natural ways to transmute our thoughts into their physical equivalent.

This power makes no attempt to discriminate between destructive thoughts and constructive thoughts. This will urge us to translate into physical reality thoughts of poverty, just as quickly as it will influence us to act upon thoughts of riches.

Our brains become magnetized with the dominating thoughts which we hold in our minds, and by means with which no man is familiar. These magnets attracts to us the forces, the people, the circumstances of life which harmonize with the nature of our dominating thoughts.

Before we can accumulate riches in great abundance, we must become "Money Conscious" until the desire for money drives us to create definite plans for acquiring it.

Every human being who reaches the age of

understanding of the purpose of money, wishes for it.

Wishing will not bring riches. But desiring riches with a state of mind that becomes an obsession, then planning definite ways and means to acquire riches and backing those plans with persistence which does not recognize failure, will bring riches.

No two minds ever come together without, thereby, creating a third, invincible, intangible force which may be likened to a third mind.

CHAPTER EIGHT

INFINITE INTELLIGENCE

It won't be incorrect if you call this Infinite Intelligence God.

HE is the power that carries out the Creative Process in the Earth, the Universe and in all Creation.

HIS purpose is Expansion and Growth. He carries out His Creative Process through the Maintenance of all Creations and the destruction of what has served its purpose in the Universe.

You can also call Infinite Intelligence "Collective Consciousness" of which individuals are all constituents as drop of water are constituents of water in the ocean.

The list of source from which power may be attained is headed by Infinite Intelligence.

When two or more people coordinate in a spirit of harmony and work toward a definite objective, they place themselves in position through that alliance to absorb power directly from the great universal storehouse of Infinite Intelligence. (Where two or three are gathered in my name, there am I in the midst of them).

This is the greatest source of power. It is the source to which every great leader turns.

The other sources from which the knowledge necessary for the accumulation of power are the five senses of man. They are not always as reliable as Infinite Intelligence which does not err.

We use our brains to manufacture our thoughts. The brain is the organ of the Conscious. It is here subjected to our power of reasoning. When the Objective Mind, our Consciousness is satisfied that the thought is true, it is sent to the Subjective Mind, our Subconscious to be made into our flesh, to be brought forth into the world as reality.

The Subconscious Mind cannot and does not argue or reason, it only acts. It accepts the conclusion of the objective mind as final.

Our Subconscious Mind has been likened to the sun of the body, because it is a Central Point of Distribution for the energy which the body is constantly generating. This energy is real energy, and this sun is real sun, and the energy is being distributed by very real nerves to all parts of the body, and is thrown off in an atmosphere which envelopes the body.

When the Subconscious Mind is in active operation and is radiating life energy and vitality to every parts of the body, and to everyone whom he meets, the sensations are pleasant; the body is filled with health and all with whom he comes in contact experience a pleasant sensation.

If there is any interruption of this radiation, the sensation becomes unpleasant, the flow of life to some parts of the body is stopped and this is the cause of every ill to the human race – Physical, Mental or Environmental.

The Creative Power is present within all of us as part of the Universal Creative Power. A part must be the same in kind and quality as the whole. This means that this creative power is absolutely unlimited as the whole.

It is not bound by precedent of any kind and consequently has no prior existing pattern by which to apply its constructive principle.

You can only tap into this magnificent Creative Power through your Subconscious Mind. This is why it is very important to build a good rapport with your Subconscious Mind.

Here is how the creative process work – First you desire something and with the proper tools you impress that idea into your Subconscious Mind.

Since your Subconscious Mind is able to download information from the Unlimited Database of the Universe, it taps into this and receives the needed information.

Once you have it in your Subconscious Mind, it either comes to your Conscious awareness like a sudden realization (intuition, inspiration etc) or you will have to deliberately work to bring it to your awareness using certain techniques.

If you have faith and believe and act on that idea, you will be amazed by the results.

Millions of people fail at this particular step – THEY FEAR TO TAKE ACTIONS.

They see things from their limited perspectives. They fail to realize that what appear as futile thing to us could be the blueprint of our success.

We all have complete access to this collective consciousness always and our Subconscious Mind is always receiving the solution to our problems.

Our aims should be to bring this information to our Conscious awareness.

Here are five suggested techniques to receive messages from the Infinite Intelligence.

1. **MEDITATION:** Thought concentrated on a definite purpose becomes power. Mentally concentrate on the object of your desire; when you are concentrating, you are impressing the Subconscious. Meditation helps you to calm down your mind and thus slows down the rate of thoughts; as a result, you will be able to receive the inspirations. The major cause of our inability to hear our inner guidance is due to the voices inside our heads. The restlessness of the mind caused by the unwanted thoughts blocks our intuitions and if we could silence our thoughts somehow, it will become easy for us to bring the message received by our Subconscious Mind from the Universal Mind to our conscious awareness.

2. **MIND EXERCISE**: Mind exercise increases your present awareness and that means you will be able to detach yourself from your thoughts more frequently. When you lessen the rate at which thoughts come to your mind, you open yourself to receive the insights that lead you to success.

3. **VISUALIZATION**: Visualization simply put, involves the use of mental imagery to

achieve a desired result. You imagine yourself doing, or being, the thing you want to do or to be successfully with repetition. For example, a tennis player wishing to improve his backhand would imagine doing it over and over in his mind with proper form. A person wishing to have financial success would imagine himself as already living the life of someone with abundant wealth. Visualization can be enhanced by use of meditation; which is maximum lucidity of thought. It creates the most conductive mindset for powerful effective mental imagery and stillness of the mind. Meditation melts the many layers of worry, anxiety, depression and fear, logging up thought processes. It gives crystal clear thinking and mind mastery, which allows you successful visualization anytime you want – making your intended goal, whether it be love, good health, wealth, more friends or success, much easier.

4. **DREAMS:** A dream is a succession of images, ideas, emotions, and sensations that usually occur involuntarily in the mind during certain stages of sleep. The content and purpose of dreams are not fully understood., though they have been topic of scientific speculation, as well as a subject of philosophical and religious interest throughout recorded history. Dream interpretation is the attempt at drawing meaning from dreams and searching for an

underlying message. Dreams mainly occur in the rapid-eye movement (REM) stage of sleep – when the brain activity is high and resembles that of being awake. REM sleep is revealed by continuous movements of the eyes during sleep. At times, dreams may occur during other stages of sleep. However, these dreams tend to be much less vivid or memorable. The length of a dream can vary, they may last for a few seconds, or approximately 20-30 minutes. People are more likely to remember the dream if they are awakened during the REM phase. The average person has three to five dreams per night, and some may have up to seven, however, most dreams immediately or quickly forgotten. Dreams tend to last as the night progresses. During a full eight-hour night sleep, most dreams occur in the typical two hours of REM. Opinions about the meaning of dreams have varied and shifted through time and culture. Dreams reveal insight into hidden desires and emotions. Dreams assist in memory formation, problem solving, or simply are a product of random brain activation. IN modern times, dreams have been seen as a connection to the unconscious mind. Dreams can have varying natures, such as being frightening, exciting, magical, melancholic, adventurous, or sexual. The events in dreams are generally outside the control of the dreamer, with the exception of lucid dreaming, where the dreamer is self-

aware. Dreams can at times make a creative thought occur to the person or give a sense of inspiration.
5. **SELF HYPNOSIS**: Self-hypnosis or autohypnosis is a form, process or result of hypnosis which is self-induced, and normally makes use of self-suggestion. Self-hypnosis can make a person more yielding than normal. Self-hypnosis is used extensively in modern hypnotherapy. It can take the form of hypnosis carried our by means of a learned routine. Hypnosis may help pain management, anxiety, depression, obesity, asthma and skin conditions. When this practice is mastered, it can improve concentration, recall, enhance problem solving, alleviate headaches and even improve one's control of emotions. Self-hypnosis require four distinct steps; **a. Motivation** – Without proper motivation, an individual will find it very difficult to practice self-hypnosis. **b. Relaxation** – The individual must be thoroughly relaxed and must set aside time to perform this act. Additionally, distractions should be eliminated as full attention is needed. **c. Concentration** – The individual needs to concentrate completely as progress is made each time the mind focuses on a single image. **d. Directing** – This is an option used only when the individual wants to work on a specific goal. The individual must direct his concentration on visualizing the desired result.

FAILURE TO THINK.

Mind in action is thought and thought is creative. Matter is powerless, passive and inert. Mind is force, energy and power. Mind shapes and controls matter.

Every form which matter takes is but the expression of some pre-existing thought. But thought works no magic transformations. It obeys natural laws, it sets in motion natural forces, it releases natural energies; it manifests in your conduct and actions, and these in turn react upon your friends and acquaintances and eventually upon the whole of your environment.

You can originate thought and since thoughts are creative, you can create for yourself the things you desire.

You can also fail to think, allowing your mind to be blank, not making use of your brain or acting as a brainless person.

When you fail to think, you limit yourself to superficial conditions and make yourself a beast of burden for those who think. Unless you are willing to think, you shall have to work, and the less you think, the more you shall have to work and the less you shall get for your work.

When you fail to think, you severe the link between the Infinite and the Finite, between the Universal and the Individual.

The period when your mind can be blank, when you do not think is very short and limited. There is no vacuum in nature and your mind is no exception. The saying "idle mind is the playground for the devil" is a scientific precision, for when the mind is blank, thoughts like flood of water rushes in like a flood to fill the mind.

The risk herein is that they should be negative thoughts of fear, lack which are destructive, but should be thought of wisdom, strength, courage and all harmonious conditions which are creative and in the path of growth.

Accurate and constructive thoughts should therefore be our goal. For with this, we can possess everything that others acquire by toil, never have to struggle with conscience as we always act correctly, conduct ourselves with tact , learn everything easily, complete everything we start with a happy knack, live in eternal harmony with ourselves without ever reflecting much on what we do or ever experiencing difficult or toil.

IT IS A GIFT FROM GOD.

In a mental hospital, the decision to admit a new intake is determined this way; Bathtub is filled with water and then the intake is given a teaspoon, a glass and a bucket. He or she will then be asked to empty the bathtub using one of the items given. A normal person would pull the drain plug. If you choose the bucket, you are not using your brain. You are not thinking.

Thought brings initiative; INITIATIVE backed by FAITH and the ZEAL to win is guaranteed SUCCESS.

CHAPTER NINE

CIRCLES OF LIFE

Of all the factors that influence a man's thought, that is, Heredity, Environments, Information, Knowledge and Experience, heredity is the only factor that does not change with age.

Our life is being governed by a Law of PERIODITY. Every that lives has periods of birth, growth, fruitage and decline. These periods are governed by Septimal Law – which relates to number seven.

This law of sevens governs the days of the week, the phases of the moon, the harmonies of sound, light, heat, electricity magnetism and the atomic structure.

It governs individual life and of nations. It also dominates the activities of the commercial world.

Life is growth and each seven years period takes us into a new circle of life.

The first seven years is the period of Infancy, the next seven, the period of Childhood representing the beginning of individual responsibility.

The next seven is Adolescence Period which is Educational Period when obedience and industry instilled into the growing mind. The forth seven years is Attainment of Full Growth. Virtue of Caution, Thrift, Charity, Magnanimity, Diligence and Prudence dominate this period.

The fifth period is the Constructive period, when men began to acquire property, possession, a home and family.

The next from 36 to 42, is a period of reconstruction, adjustment and recuperation, so as to be ready for the next circle of seven beginning with the 50th year.

CIRCLES OF LIFE.

1st 7 years **INFANCY**
1-7

2nd 7 years **CHILDHOOD** Irresponsible
8 – 14 Representing the
Beginning of
Individual responsibility.

3rd 7 years **ADOLESCENCE** Educational
PERIOD Period
15 – 21 Obedience, Industry
Instilled into the
Growing mind.

4th 7 years **ATTAINMENT** Virtue of caution,
22 – 28 **OF FULL** Thrift, Charity,
GROWTH Magnanimity,
Diligence, Prudence.

5th 7 years **CONSTRUCTIVE** Practical Period
29 – 35 **PERIOD** of life. Wealth

	Men acquire property, Possession, Home & Family. Filled with Business Activities.	Wealth become an object. Responsibility Grows. Duties Of life heavier. Social side Prospered.
6th 7 years 36 – 42	**PERIOD OF REACTION AND CHANGES**	More Social side expresses prosperity.
7th 7 years 43 – 49	**PERIOD OF RECONSTRUCTION ADJUSTMENT AND RECUPERATION**	Glory of man-hood, Fullness of Motherhood. Turns to wider Interest.
8th 7 years 50 – 56		Virtue of Equilibrium, Justice, Strength, Courage, Vigour and Generosity.
60 UPWARD	Virtue of last Three circles made Manifest as patience, Self- sacrifice, Services, Parity,	Experience garnered, Lesson of life stored for ego. Wisdom, Tender-filling

Wisdom, Gentleness of sympathy to
And compassion. All.

IT IS MAN'S CAPACITY TO THINK THAT MAKES HIM A CREATOR INSTEAD OF A CREATURE.

CHAPTER TEN

THE WORLD AT LARGE.

Just as man grow from being a child to an adolescent, from an adolescent to a young adult, from a young adult to an adult and then grow into old age, so the world has its evolutionary stages as well.

There are evolutionary stages in societies. There are evolutionary in families. And the world has its own evolutionary process.

Because humanity now spans your world, at least the surface of your world, and has gained a relative degree of control of the world with great risks, it is important now for you to know that you are entering into a new era.

It is not a new age, for an age is a very long time. This is a period of transition, which will be difficult and turbulent. Its opportunities and demands will be tremendous. Its risk of failure will be substantial. It is not a time for the faint of heart or for the weak minded. It is not a time for the ambivalent or the self-indulgent.

It is a time for great strength and dedication. Knowledge within you will give you this strength and determination as you become a student of Knowledge, as you advance in The Way of Knowledge and as you take the steps to Knowledge. This is because you are needed for something great in this life.

Do not compare your purpose with the purpose of your ancestors. Do not think that your purpose is the same as someone's a thousand years ago or five hundred years ago or even one hundred years ago.

Your purpose is related to the needs of the world and the circumstances of the world.

Ultimately, everyone's purpose serves the reclamation and the preservation of Knowledge in the world. However, what you may end up doing may seem very different from this, if only in appearance. It is the spirit with which you give, the quality of your gift and the quality of your awareness and your relationships that will keep Knowledge alive in the world.

Everything else that is accomplished is to help people, to serve people, to heal people, to enable people, to strengthen people and to take care of people.

The need for knowledge will grow dramatically. There are so many people in the world that have so little, and there are so few that have so much. The resources of the world are shrinking, and the problems of the world are growing. This is seemingly a terrible situation when you put it all together, but it is just the kind of situation that will call people into action – not just an individual here and there who is inspired, but greater numbers of people.

The world will be calling them out of their self-preoccupation. The world will be calling them out of their personal interest and tragedies. The world will be demanding things of them.

This is what calls your purpose out of you. Do not think you can go off and meditate all day every day and find your purpose. You must go into the world and have it brought out of you. The world represents a relationship in which your purpose is initiated, fostered and realized.

That is why seeking escape from the world or a permanent retreat from the world is counterproductive. The very tribulations in the world that you find so difficult and so unpleasant are the very things that will call out of you the greatness that you have come to give. Do not, then, condemn the world when in fact it creates the right conditions for your redemption.

The world's emergence into the New World will be the greatest transition humanity has ever faced. This is understandable because humanity is a very recent race. Yes, the primitive life of your ancestors went on for a very long time, mainly because your world is such an easy world to live in compared to other worlds. However, the demands of life now are much greater, and the pace of life is much faster.

That is because the evolution of the world is accelerating. It is accelerating because of the global population of humanity, it is accelerating because of the global problems of humanity and it is accelerating because of the presence of New World forces in the world.

What kind of change will this great transition produce? Fundamentally, it will change how people view their place in the world and their position in the larger arena of life called the New World.

We introduce the idea of the New World so that you can begin to think about this greater context of life and begin to understand and accept it as a governing fact of your life. It represents your destiny. It contains a greater set of influence and represents a greater set of problems, challenges and opportunities that awaits you.

This is why your technology is racing ahead. Some of this technology was introduced from the New World in order to accelerate your development.

Much of it was your own creation. It is headed in a certain direction. That is why you cannot stand still, confused about yourself, involved with your thoughts, lost in your wishes or buried in your fears.

Life is moving quickly. You must move too. You must become attentive and aware. You must have an open mind, an attentive mind, a watchful mind and a careful mind, but not a fearful mind.

As humanity's idea of itself changes, its social institutions and structures will change as well. Fundamentally, you will begin to see yourself as a member of your world, not simply as a member of a nation or of a group or of a religion or of a culture or of an extended family or of a political persuasion.

All of these things will be overshadowed by the presence of the New World, which will make them increasingly insignificant.

As these realization is passed from one generation to another, national interest will change, with a greater emphasis on interdependence with other nations and on mutual survival and well-being.

Indeed, even if New World forces were not present in the world, the overshadowing of your world's problems would generate this. Only it would happen much more slowly and with less likelihood of a good result because humanity would fight against itself over who gets the last of the resources, who gets the last of the benefits and who gets the greatest share and so forth.

The evolution of the world is casting a greater shadow over humanity and a greater difficult, but a difficulty that can redeem the world and unite its population, a difficulty that can put everyone in the same boat and give everyone the same problem. Where, then, will you look for help?

You may look to God, but God will point you towards one another. Therefore, you must look towards one another. "How can we work together? How can we work together to strengthen and to unify our race and to secure and to balance our world?"

This won't be merely an altruistic wish. It will become a vital necessity. It will be something everyone has to think about. And those who refuse to do so will work against humanity at large and will generate conflict and discord.

This is why you must be forward thinking now and not backward thinking. You must not think about preserving the securities and the ideals that you have clung to before. You must keep pace with life in order to benefit from life and to give to life.

In this way, you will not become one of life's causalities but one of its benefactors. In this way, your vital years will be given in service to the progress of the world, rather than being a hindrance to this progress.

Many people and even nations of people will struggle against the change that is coming. They will try to preserve their interests and their identities to the exclusion of the world's interest and identity. This will produce great friction.

However, as your world community slowly comes together, with much discord, there will be a greater feeling of consensus. World opinion will have greater impact, even before a world government is established.

World government is inevitable. It will happen. It will happen in order to regulate commerce. It will happen in order to prevent crime and starvation. It will happen in order to preserve the environment which different nations share. It will happen in order to regulate the quality of the larger natural resources which everyone shares, like water and air.

The creation of world government will be difficult. It will be fraught with great tribulation and conflict. But it will happen because it is your destiny. If you fail in this regard, you will fail even to meet your world's needs, and this will overtake you in time. You cannot afford this, and you know it

This is a great opportunity for people to step beyond their personal interests and to gain a greater perspective on life, and with it a greater sense of purpose.

Never think that your purpose will arise from what you want for yourself. People make this mistake every day. They think "Well, my purpose? Let's see, what do I want?" as if they were choosing from a great wish list.

Purpose has to do with what the world needs from you and what you are able to give to the world, which may or may not conform to your personal goals, plans and ambitions.

The world's emergence into the New World will change your understanding of religion. Here, there will be great difficulty and tremendous resistance. Most religions of the world are based on an anthropocentric view of the universe. Consequently, as the presence of New World forces in the world becomes more obvious and apparent, more acceptable and more generally recognized, people will either yield to a larger viewpoint and open themselves to re-evaluate their ideas and their fundamental beliefs, or they will try to reassert their religious ideas, thinking that they are in the right and that the rest of the universe somehow is in the wrong.

They will think that they are blessed and guided by their religious faith, while the rest of the universe has either been spiritually denied or has been too foolish to respond.

Human arrogance will demonstrate itself here in all of its destructive manifestations. You will see this, and your children will see this .

The inability of people to respond to the present and to the future because of their fixed ideas and their past referencing will create tremendous conflict.

The world's emergence into the New World is a great challenge in and of itself, but what will be more burdensome will be human response or lack of it.

No one wants to give up his or her pleasure. No one wants to yield his or her beliefs. No one wants to sacrifice those things that seems validate them. No one wants to close a chapter on his or her personal history. No one wants to do these things unless of course they are students of Knowledge, who will give these things up freely and set them asides in order to face life anew.

However, for those who are not students of Knowledge, which will be most of the people in the world, this will be a tremendous confrontation. In fact, it will be a series of tremendous confrontations.

CHAPTER ELEVEN

MORE WORLD AT LARGE.

Destiny must move you forward, whether you are willing or not, whether you can yield or not, whether you can learn or not.

The results of destiny are in your hands, but the process itself is not.

Whether the world's emergence into the New World has a good result for humanity or a devastating result is up to you, but your emergence will happen either way.

The challenges ahead require a new approach, a new understanding and a greater sense of identity and purpose in life.

Here it will be very difficult for people to face the fact that their future will not be like the past and that they cannot use the past as a reference in determining the future.

They must meet things face to face, head on. This is a great challenge but this is what redeems people. This is what elevates a race. This is what calls upon human wisdom, ingenuity, skill, dedication and cooperation. Only a greater set of problems can do this for you now.

Otherwise, without them, humanity will slowly sink under the weight of its own conflicts, its own indulgences and its own violence. Everything will deteriorate. Everyone will become poorer and more desperate.

The answer is in the heavens, in the New World. Look to the heavens for inspiration. Look to the New World. Heaven itself is beyond the New World, but the New World is where you will instinctively look for the answer. Your world needs this emergence into the New World. It is not simply that it is your destiny. It also represents a great answer to a great need.

However, it is not an answer that was recently given. It is an answer that was given when the world began.

The evolution of life in the world is a part of the evolution of life in the New World. It cannot be apart from this. That is why your future, your destiny and the greater context for understanding yourself individually will all be found in the New World.

Human religion, human society and human culture are all based upon the past, and this will work against you.

However, your natural inclinations for spirituality, for social cooperation and productivity, for political stability and for justice and equanimity will prepare you for the future and enable you to do whatever needs to be done in order to advance and to bring a greater order, peace and justice into the world.

It will not be a perfect order, but it must be a greater order. It will not be a perfect peace, but it must be a greater peace. It will not be a perfect justice but it must be a greater justice.

Humanity must become united, even with all of its diversity, because humanity is one race in the New World. The distinctions that you make to separate yourself from others are meaningless to your visitors, except insofar as these distinctions can be exploited. They represent your weakness, not your strength.

You are emerging from tribalism in the world. The tribes now are very large, and many of them have technological power, but the mentality that governs their behaviour has not yet full changed. To work for your clan – to work for your group alone, to strike out against others or everyone – is mindless and senseless and will not work in a new world.

You are indeed, in the process of creating a new world. Old institutions will fade. Old religions will have to expand and adapt or they will die out. Old faiths will have to be given new passion or they will disappear with each new generation. Old cultural bonds will fade, as they must.

You cannot live now to honour your parents or their parents. You must live to meet the requirements of life as it is now. There will be much error . There will be grievous error. Humanity as a whole has never learned anything of a larger magnitude in a graceful way, but your adaptability is still significant.

Your creative ability is still significant. Your mobility in the world is still significant. The world still has the resources to enable you to grow and to adapt to the New World, in contrast to many other worlds where the resources were depleted or were never abundant to begin with. As your natural resources fade, your technology will have to advance.

Let us, then, look into your future to see how things might be. This is not a future that is way ahead of your time, but a future that you will experience and are beginning to taste even now.

First of all, everyone will become much poorer, and there will have to be more sharing. The number of people who possess great wealth will diminish compared to society at large, and there will have to be more sharing.

Your natural environment will become increasingly polluted, so much so that there will be whole arrears of the world where people cannot live. People will take to living indoors more and more and will even explore the possibilities of living underground.

Food production will be greatly affected, and new methods will have to be established. New forms of religious expression and experience will be generated in order to be relevant to the times which you will face. National problems will split over into other nations increasingly, requiring international intervention and cooperation to a greater degree.

Many people will starve, for there will not be enough food to go around to meet crisis situations. This will generate a national and international network of food production and distribution. You will need to get used to living with less – fewer possessions, fewer opportunities and less mobility.

These are general things which we are describing. You can sense them in the world now, and you will feel them growing as time goes on.

Can you change all this? You can only adapt to changing conditions and use them to improve the condition of humanity and the condition of your mind.

THINK OUT YOUR DESTINY

The present and the future will require a new mind, not an old mind. They will require a new response, not an old response. They will require human invention, rather than human indolence. They will require greater and greater adaptation and adjustment.

They will challenge old forms of thinking and behaviour. All of this is necessary, and it is beneficial. It is beneficial because it is necessary. And it is necessary because this is the evolution of the world. Humanity has grown too big and too powerful. It is having too great an impact on its own environment to continue without self-control, without Wisdom and without the sense of world community and world responsibility.

Destiny will utterly change your life. You have come to serve a world in transition. It will feel like a whole new age is starting, but it is simply because an old age is dying. A world in transition needs great human ingenuity and courage, which will emanate from Knowledge within you.

You are destined to gain contact with other forms of intelligent life from the New World. Some will oppose you, some will abuse you, some will ignore you and some will attempt to establish a relationship with you.

Each of them will offer a different kind of challenge and a different requirement. At this time, many people still think that the universe is a great, empty place. "Oh yes, there is life out there somewhere, but certainly it must be sparse, and it is all for the taking".

In the future, you will go out and attempt to set your flags down in any world that you can reach, but the New World will tempt your ambitions and your desire for conquest. Even your need for new resources will be curtailed because you will find that the New World is indeed full of activity, particularly in this regions of space where you live. And you will find that the regions that you seek to claim for yourself have already been claimed.

This will require that you learn about the New World and develop Wisdom and diplomacy within a large context of life. These are skill which your race will benefit from skills which will temper your ambition and increase your responsibility.

Not only are your visitors technologically advanced, they have greater social cohesion, or they would not have been able to reach your shores. They are coming into a world where tribal warfare is dominant, where one human being cannot recognize another, where anyone claims different allegiances and authorities.

They are coming into a world where people are fearful, superstitious and self-indulgent and where there is great tragedy, suffering and human abuse.

How would this world look to you if you were a visitor coming here for the first time? Even with your human viewpoint, you can gain a perspective of how you must look to those who are visiting. Will they be compassionate towards you? Will they attempt to help you? Will they attempt to avoid you? Will they want to have a relationship with you? Can they trust you? Can you be relied upon? Are you consistent enough in order to establish relations?

THINK OUT YOUR DESTINY

These are all meaningful questions for you to ask in order to gain a New World perspective, even from a human point of view. Seeing yourself from a New World perspective will show you what you must accomplish and what your great disabilities are at this time. This will give you a new understanding of yourself, one that is very fair and honest.

Life is requiring a greater evolution for humanity at this time. Your own life is moving quickly because life in general is moving quickly. You cannot escape this. Move to the most peaceful part of the world, and everything you do will still be affected.

Do not run and hide. Prepare. Do not deny and avoid. Prepare. Do not argue against reality; do not repudiate reality. Prepare for reality. The coming of the New World is the great threshold for humanity. You must prepare.

The world needs a new awareness, a new approach and a new foundation for society. You must prepare.

You are now at the beginning of the transition. The generations ahead are all part of this transition. You will need to lay down the foundation for what is to come. And yet is this not what you came here to do? This is what you came here to do – to lay down the foundation for life to come so that future generations may flourish here and be abundant.

The preparation cannot be left only in the hands of one or two saintly or wonderful people. It must be a responsibility that is felt throughout the population. People must not look at the change ahead and say, "Well, how can I benefit? How can I keep what I have? How can I make more money? That is mindless and destructive. What you will be facing will be too dire for that kind of approach. Everyone must feel this responsibility.

Everyone must take it upon himself or herself to do something in concert with others – something productive, something constructive, something that transcends his or her own personal interests. Everyone will not do this, of course, but more people need to prepare.

You need to prepare. You prepare through the New World Way of Knowledge. This is the only preparation for the New World. The New World will also prepare you to meet the world's difficulties and tribulations.

It will prepare you to face and experience the dying of an old age and the difficult emergence and transition into a new life. It will enable you to go from an old mind to a new mind, from an old approach to life to a new approach to life, from an old experience of relationships to a new experience of relationships.

The preparation makes this possible because it enables you to build your life on Knowledge and not on the substitutes for Knowledge.

Humanity is destined to become a part of the New World. This is its evolution. This is its destiny. This is where you are headed. This is what you must contend with. And this is what you must now prepare yourself for – emotionally, psychologically, intellectually and spiritually.

Do not protect your old traditions. Prepare for change. If you protect the past, you will feel that life is assaulting you, and you will fight against it. You will become violent and become an antagonist in life.

You have only three responses to reality. You can go towards it, you can go away from it or you can go against it. Go towards your future. Go towards the present. Find that strength within yourself that enables you to do this, the strength which is born of Knowledge within you. Find the desire to be in a changing world, the desire that is born of Knowledge. Let change take its course, but contribute to it for the good because your contribution is needed.

You cannot be left out. If you do not contribute, you will have failed in life, and you will go home to your Spiritual Family with your gift unopened. There you will not be punished, but you will feel great regret, and your life here will be seen as unfulfilling and unfulfilled.

You are destined to learn from the New World, but first, you must survive in the New World and contend with the New World.

In the New World, there are races at all levels of evolution and technological skill. There are races that are dedicated to good. And there are races that are dedicated to destruction. However, because they have to contend with each other, they moderate each other. To the extend that they do have contact, they learn from each other and influence each other, physically and mentally.

If you can see yourself from outside the world looking in, you will begin to get an understanding of how they might approach you, what they might want and what they might think to be possible.

We will give you a few ideas now to consider regarding the intentions of your visitors. These intentions may not hold true for all of them, but these ideas should still be a prime concern for you.

The first concern is the preservation of your natural environment. That is a prime concern because in the New World natural environments such as yours are considered resources that cannot be destroyed. The need for biological regeneration elsewhere and the abundance of biological resources here make your world too valuable to be destroyed. It will not be allowed for you to destroy it.

Should you proceed heedlessly, then there will be intervention, and your race will be controlled. This would be very unfortunate. It would be unfortunate because you will not have learned what you must learn. It would be unfortunate because you will have given up your authority and self-determination because you were unwilling to exercise them properly. It would be unfortunate because the opportunity to advance your race would have been missed. It would be unfortunate because your freedom would be lost. Losing all of these is a possibility. And it is largely up to you.

Your neighbours and visitors are also concerned with your aggressive behaviour. It will not be allowed for you to set out on a mission of conquest, even in the local universe. You do not know what you are dealing with. It is a more matured environment out there. You are like the young adolescent, brash and full of yourself, with newfound powers and abilities but without the wisdom to know how they are to be used and without the restraint necessary to prevent you from using them against yourself or others. In this you must mature, and gaining this maturity is essential.

Contact with the New World will temper your ambitions. And ir will give you a different kind of perspective about life. The universe is yours to share and to learn from. You will be encountering races far more advanced than you and with very different temperaments. If you are to contend with them successfully, you must learn to contend with your own kind successfully.

The differences between you and them will be great, just as the differences between you and other human beings are small. If you cannot establish harmony where the differences are small, how can you establish harmony where the differences are great?

God's eternal plan is having creations and kingdoms which are willingly subject to Him and consecrated to the same end that He is consecrated to;
"THE HIGHEST GOOD OF BEING FOR ALL".

CHAPTER TWELVE

AGES AND WORLD DISPENSATIONS

Ages means the length of time. It is any period of time whether long or short. A Season.

Dispensation is a Political, Religious or Social system prevailing at a particular time.

We will confine our discussion to the religious dispensation, which is a divinely ordained system prevailing at a particular period of history.

Dispensation in this context refers to a moral or probationary period in Angelic or Human history, during which time God dealt with Angels or Men according to a particular test or responsibility, under which each was to remain true to his trust of administering affair for God under His direction.

Each dispensation has its own particular beginning and ending; each is characterized by distinctive principles of God's dealings; each has a favourable beginning; each has a definite test; and each ends in failure and judgment except the final and eternal one.

In each, God has a definite and different immediate purpose, all working towards the ultimate purpose of ridding the universe of all rebellions so that all free moral agents will be willingly and eternally subject to God, Christ and the Holy Ghost, as originally planned with God All-in-All forever.

There are 9 dispensations in the Scripture; 7 of these are men's probationary periods and these came between 2 other periods – the dispensation of Angels (the Ante Chaotic Age) and the dispensation of Faithful Angels and the Redeemed.

1. **DISPENSATION OF ANGELS**.

From the Ageless to Defeat of Satan.

It is called Dispensation of Angels because Angels, not men, were given ruler-ship under God to administer the will of God and rule the earth and other planets.

1. **Length**: From the time the earth was created in the presence of Angels to the time of chaos and defeat of Satan in his invasion of heaven.
2. **Beginning**; Every Angels, devil and man of all the principalities and powers were sinless to begin with. Lucifer, the ruling cherub of earth was described as 'perfect in thy ways from the day that thou was created till iniquity was found in thee'. With everything perfect, h had a most favourable beginning and could have remained so, had he not exalted himself in an effort to dethrone God.
3. **Test**: the test for Angelic rulers was the same as for man; to be subjected to God and obey Him in all that He commanded.

   Lucifer and all Angels had ways to walk in or they could not have sinned. Sin is transgression of the law, for Angels as well as men.
4. **Purpose of God in Testing and the Means**

Used: God's purpose is to test Angels to see if they would remain true to Him before using them eternally as trusted servants. God used the ways He restricted the Angels to walk in as the means of testing them.
5. **Failure**: Some Angelic beings failed to continue in the truth and the ways God made clear to them. Over one third rebelled including Lucifer. God found it necessary to charge them for folly, sin and rebellion.
6. **Judgment**: God prepared hell for the devil and his Angels. Some are in hell now. Lucifer and those still loose with him will eventually be put into hell. Immediate judgment came by their defeat and God took away from them their ruler-ship. They are now pseudo-rulers of earth because of Adam's fall and submitted to them. Man now in Christ has power over them.
7. **God's Provision of Redemption**: In what way God offered reconciliation to Angels and how many availed themselves of His Grace is not revealed. The Bible is not history about Angels but about Man.

2. DISPENSATION OF INNOCENCE

Duration unknown but ends at Adam's fall.

So called because man was tested and put on probation while in innocence. He has not sinned.

1. **Length**: The length is not known. Judging by Satan's action, he tried to cause the fall of man immediately. The dispensation might have lasted less than a week.
2. **Beginning**: Everything was perfect, sinless and under man's dominion, with just one command to obey
3. **Test**: Not to eat of the tree of |Knowledge of Good and Evil.
4. **Purpose of God in Testing and Means Used**: To see if man would remain innocent and true to His trust under perfect condition. God tested him before he had offspring, so that if he sinned, the entire race could be dealt with through the same means of Grace which offers redemption to all who desire it, and promises eternal separation from God for all who fail to seek reconciliation. The means God used was the tree of the Knowledge of Good and Evil, together with the temptation of Satan, to see if man would remain true.
5. **Failure**: The Fall. The fall of Adam
6. **Judgment**: Because of his sin, man reaped separation from God, fellowship and union with Satan, and demons, power to do evil and be evil, unclean lust and habits, unbelief, hardship, sufferings, hell, eternal damnation, and other curses too numerous to mention. Man became depraved, obstinate and rebellious, lustful, evil continuously, full of abominations and blind in mind.
7. **God's Provision of Redemption**: God promised a Redeemer who would come and

restore man's dominion.

3. DISPENSATION OF CONSCIENCE.
From Adam's Fall to Noah's Flood.

Called dispensation of Conscience because man was tested to see if he would obey his conscience regarding right and wrong. There were no written laws. The Ten Commandments had not been given to Adams in the previous dispensation. His only law was not to eat of the tree of the Knowledge of Good and Evil; and after being driven out of the garden of Eden, he ceased to have that law.

This is man's age of freedom, for man was free to do as he pleased until it became necessary for God to interfere.

1. **Length**: From Adam's fall to 600th years of Noah. (1656 years)
2. **Beginning**: A new beginning altogether. Inhabitants had Knowledge of God and a new covenant with God.
3. **Test**: Obedience to the dictates of Conscience as to right and wrong.
4. **Purpose of God in Testing and Means Used**: Since man knew good and evil now, purpose was to guide him in the proper exercise of his conscience to do the right and refuse the wrong; to teach fallen man that only by obedience to God could he be restored to his original dominion and get rid

of the curse; and to test man under freedom of conscience without restraining or compulsion to see if he would voluntarily choose right from wrong and give service to Him instead of Satan.

If voluntary righteousness was rejected, then God planned to add laws and punishments to enforce obedience for man's own good. God wanted man to see that in his fallen state he could not choose the best good of being and of the universe, and that he was powerless to cope with the innumerable fallen angels and demons with whom he had now entered into voluntary union through sin, and who sought his eternal damnation.

God wanted man to be brought to helplessness in himself so that he would turn to Him for help, grace and power against sin, Satan, fallen angels, demon, sickness and suffering in the struggle to overcome the curse. He wanted man to know that He was the only true friend and helper and that only through Him was there a way out of sin and the curse and an opportunity for restoration to original damnation.

God's means to bring man to a place of utter dependence upon Him for help and redemption from the curse was the conscience, freedom of the will without restraint and compulsion to choose right or wrong and malice of the devil.

The conscience demonstrated how exceedingly sinful man would become if he choose evil instead of good; the full freedom of action demonstrated how far man would go in his rebellion against God before it would be necessary for Him to interfere for the good of His own eternal plan; and the malice of Satanic forces demonstrated the contrast between the two masters whom man might serve while on probation.

Such freedom of the will and conscience was what man choose in the fall; and so God permitted him to go to the full limit of wickedness that he might learn the folly of his own choice and that all coming generation might profit thereby.

5. **Failure**: All men in general failed including Adam, Cain, Cain's descendants, Seth's descendants and the daughters of men who sinned with fallen angels seeking to do away with pure Adamite stock through whom the seed of the woman was to come.
6. **Judgment**: the flood of Noah.
7. **God's provision of Redemption**: God's Grace and Mercy in sparing man to have another chance and to continue in God's eternal plan for him on the earth, the preservation of clean animals for sacrifice so as to continue faith in the coming Redeemer were provision for man's redemption after the flood.

Men in those days were actually saved by Grace through faith in the coming Redeemer who has already come.

KAYODE ENIRAIYETAN

4. **DISPENSATION OF HUMAN GOVT.**
From Noah's fall to Call of Abraham @ 70

This is called dispensation of Human government because human laws and government were instituted to regulate man's life after a long age of freedom of Conscience. God now gave Noah certain laws to govern the race by, and man was held responsible for self-government.

This dispensation ushered in the first civil laws since Adam. Some of these 7 laws have formed the basis of Human Laws in all ages since.

1. **Length:** From Noah's flood to the call of Abraham when years old. In all 427 years.
2. **Beginning**: Man was rich in experience, wisdom, had true worship, new laws, new covenant, promise of blessing, dominion of the earth, and responsibility to rule himself forever.
3. **Test**: To obey the law of Human Government, rule faithfully, punish criminals, consecrate to God and Worship Him.
4. **Purpose of God in Testing and Means Used**: To test man under a new standard of conduct. He had failed to live right without laws and the threat of punishment, now he was forced to obey the right and reject the wrong. The means God used was the various laws that were given and government was established by God, with man now being responsible to rule for the goal of all.
5. **Failure**: Noah failed, ham failed, daughters of

men at the second eruption of fallen angels in their efforts to do away with pure Adamite stock through whom the seed of the woman was to come also failed. Man in general failed. Pride, self-gratification and hero worship became prevalent in this age.

6. **Judgment**: God confused the language of men to scatter them over all the face of the earth before it was divided. About 340 years after the flood, God divided the earth into Continents and Islands as it is today, to separate the different people more permanently.

7. **God's Provision of Redemption**: faith in the coming Redeemer and the Gospel and Sacrifices typifying these truth.

5. DISPENSATION OF PROMISE

From Abraham' call to Exodus from Egypt.

So called because of promises and covenants made with Abraham and his seeds. In this period, God began to predict and emphasize the coming of the seed of the woman to be through a particular branch of the race. Now Abraham's seed was designated as the special line through whom Christ should come.

1. **Length:** From Abraham's call at 75 years of age to the exodus from Egypt. 430 years.
2. **Beginning:** God now began to deal with a special branch of the race (Abraham's seed) in the fulfillment of His plan.

    God not only promised that the Messiah should come through them, but that the promised land would be given to them eternally as a base for world missionary and governmental operations. Also that revelation of God should come through them.
3. **Test**: For Abraham and his seed, the test was to have faith in God, obey Him, remain separated from all other nations, and evangelize the world.
4. **Purpose of God in testing and Means Used:** To use one man through whom Messiah should come. To use him and his seed as God's representatives in the earth, and to give them Canaan as a base of operation concerning His program among

men in the gospel and in government eternally.

The second eruption of Son's of God among men had already begun and giants were being born. They were beginning to possess the very land God had in mind for His own headquarters on earth. God's plan was to use the Sword of Israel to destroy these giants so as to preserve a pure line for Messiah to come through. God allowed Abraham's offspring to become a great and mighty nation down in Egypt.

It was His further purpose to show the heathen through Abraham's seed, the difference between serving Him and other gods, and to make Israel an example to all men physically, mentally, morally, spiritually and financially as a nation enjoying the blessing of the true God so that others should be won to Him by such benefits.

Never was the purpose of God expressed more fully and clearly to any people; and never before did a nation have in their power such means of blessing to all nations about universal peace, prosperity and eternal salvation as Israel.

God's call of Abraham, the covenants and promises and the personal dealings of God were His means in fulfilling His plan with Israel.

5. **Failure**: Failure of Abraham, failure of Isaac, Failure of Jacob, Failure of the sons of Jacob. Failure of Israel after the death of Jacob and

sons.
6. **Judgment:** Bondage in Egypt; the beginning of oppression by the Gentiles to be carried on eventually by 8 world Kingdoms.
The judgment upon Israel was the 10 plagues.
7. **God's Provision of Redemption:** Israel had the Gospel, and the typical program of sacrifices which in shadow taught them of redemption through the Messiah.

6. DISPENSATION OF LAW

From Exodus from Egypt to Preaching of Kingdom of Heaven by John the Baptist.

So called because of the law given to Moses which became part of the rule of faith and practice during the period between Moses and Christ.

Men of this dispensation had the Gospel also.

1. **Length**: From the exodus from Egypt to the preaching of the Kingdom of Heaven by John the Baptist or from Moses to Christ (1,718 years).
2. **Beginning**: Not since the fall of man had any people experienced a more favourable beginning than Israel at the beginning of Dispensation of Law. They saw the power of God in signs and wonders in Egypt and the wilderness. He made personal appearances to them and spoke to them with audible voice. There were visible manifestations of His presence day and night. He took sickness from

them and gave them the riches of Egypt. He gave them revelations and a complete code of laws. He made covenants with them and gave them the Gospel.
3. **Test**: To obey the laws of Moses in every details.
4. **Purpose of God in Testing and Means Used**: To test Israel and see if they will obey Him. To begin commonwealth of nations headed by Israel and governed by men of His own choice. To establish a visible system of worship that would picture the coming redemptive truths in every details. To bring about the complete destruction of the giant races by the Sword of Israel so as to bring the Messiah into the world through pure Adamite Stock. To give Israel His complete revelation for the whole human race which, according to His promise to Abraham, Isaac and Jacob, would make them a blessing to all nations. God's purpose in giving the law was that the whole world might become guilty before Him and every mouth be stopped. The means God use were; Giving of the law, the completion of the organization of Israel to destroy the giant race, the settling of Israel in the promised land to use them there as an outstanding nation showing forth the benefits of serving the true God.
5. **Failure**: They failed in the wilderness through murmuring. They failed under Joshua, They failed under Judges, They failed under Kings – Nearly all the Kings of Israel and Judah

failed after the division of the Kingdom, and the people went into such apostasy that the nation was brought into captivity.

They failed under captivities. They failed in restoration from captivity.

They failed in rejecting their own Messiah and the Gospel.

6. **Judgment:** Twofold. 1. Judgment of the sins of Israel and of the whole world in the cross of Christ. 2. Judgment on Israel as a nation. The Kingdom of God was taken from them. The nation was rejected to be desolate until the 2nd advent of Christ, and it was completely destroyed in AD70 with survivors being scattered among the other nations.

7. **God's Provision of Redemption**: In the cross, God provided the true source of redemption. Up to this time, men offered sacrifice of animals as a picture of true sacrifice at Calvary.

God sent His son to take the place of all men in death, so that they might be fully redeemed, reconciled and restored to the original dominion.

7. DISPENSATION OF GRACE.

From Preach of Kingdom of Heaven by John to 2nd Advent of Christ.

So called because of the fullness of Grace brought by Jesus Christ. Men had Grace in all previous ages, but not in fullness. The same was true of laws. Men had laws in all periods of Moses, but the fullness of law came by Him.

1. **Length**: From the preaching of the Kingdom of heaven by John the Baptist to the 2nd Advent of Jesus Christ.
2. **Beginning**: Satan was defeated on the cross and made powerless to overcome any believer who would put the whole Armour of God and resist him.

No difference was made between Jew or gentile in this matter. The Dispensation of Grace began with the ministries of power – that of Christ, John the Baptist, the Apostles and other men endowed to perform miracles, as recorded in the Gospels and Acts.

It began with complete grace, promises of the fullness of the Spirit and a full commission to represent God and do the works of Christ. There is now no limitation to the belie regarding what he wants from God according to the promises.

Everyone is privileged to receive according to

his faith.
3. **Test:** Obedience to the faith of the Gospel in all its teaching.
4. **Purpose of God in Testing and Means Used**: To save all who will believe to call out a people for His name, and to build the church.
5. **Failure**: 3 fold. 1. Failure of Israel in their rejection of John, Jesus, and the Apostles; in the cruxification of their Messiah, and in war on the early Church. The Gospel first went to Israel but they would not obey, so it was taken from them and given to Gentiles. 2. The early church began to fail God in the very beginning. All the Apostles reveal divisions, strife, heresies, unclean living, false leaders and other evidences of backsliding and fallacy. 3. The Post Apostolic Church continued in failure – not evangelizing the world not living clean, not preaching the full truth or being one as Christ had prayed. The church entered the dark ages when Popes and Bishops lorded it over civil rules and murdered millions who would not conform to organized religion.

A reformation finally took place and Christianity has now been revived in part as in the New Testament, but the Church as a whole is still slow to recognize its full rights and privileges in the Gospel.

6. **Judgment:** For their rejection of John, Jesus and the early Disciples, Israel was destroyed as a nation in AD 70 and scattered among the other nations. They will not be restored until the 2nd Advent of Christ. This dispensation will end with great apostasy. Judgment will include the greatest tribulation ever known on earth. Because men will not receive the truth, God will send strong delusions to damn such rebels.
7. **God's Provision of Redemption**: The provision for this period and every other one is the death of Christ on the cross.

Men in previous dispensations had to look forward to it by faith in order to receive the benefits of the cross. Men now have to look back to it in faith to receive its benefits.

God sent His son to take the place of all men in death, so that all who would believe might be fully redeemed, reconciled and restored to original dominion.

8. **DISPENSATION OF DIVINE GOVERNMENT** (Millennium) From 2nd Advent to Beginning of New Heaven. (1000 years).

So called because Divine Government will take over all human government. The first 1,000 years of theocracy or God's rule on earth is called "The Millennium", meaning 1000 years.

1. **Length**: From the Second Advent of Christ, the Battle of Armageddon, the Judgment of Nations and the binding of Satan to the loosing of Satan, the 2nd Resurrection, The Great White Throne Judgment, the Renovation of the Heaven and Earth, and the beginning of the New Heaven and the New Earth – 1000 years.

2. **Beginning**: For the fist time since Adam submitted to Lucifer, his fallen angels and the demons, man will be free from them and have perfect earth conditions in every respect as before the fall, except that he will be subject to death for one thing – committing any sin that carry the death penalty.

   Natural and depraved instincts, tendencies and lusts will yet be a part of man's nature, but his opportunities for overcoming them will be greater because there will be no satanic power or influence, no sickness, disease, pain, or other bodily disorder.

   Christ and resurrected Saints will be reigning over the coming generations from the beginning of the Millennium and forever.

3. **Test**: To obey Christ, Resurrected Saints, Civil and Religious Laws of the Kingdom, and conform to the Will of God.
4. **Purpose of God in Testing and Means Used**: To put down rebellion on earth, fulfill the everlasting covenants of the past; vindicate and avenge Christ and the Saints, exalt Resurrected saints of all ages to a Kingly and Priestly position, judge the Nations in Righteousness and restore the earth to its rightful owners, restore Israel as the head of all nations, and to put all enemies under the feet of Christ so as to bring back the perfect conditions that existed before the fall of Lucifer and Adam – This is the purpose of God in the dispensation of Divine Government or the Millennium.

    Means God will use is to send Jesus Christ, faithful Angels, and Resurrected saints from heaven to put down rebellion on earth. He will complete His testing period for man, and remove the curse.
5. **Failure**: As in all 6 previous dispensations, there will be some who will not choose God and Righteousness. At the end of the Millennium, multitudes will follow the devil who will be loosed from the bottomless pit in order to give men a final opportunity to rebel openly and try to overthrow God's government.
6. **Judgment**: Fire will come down from heaven and devour the earth rebels who have lived through the 1000years or part of it, if they are

born within the period, and who chose Satan rather than God. Thus, God will bring to an end the rebellion in His Universal kingdom which began with Lucifer, unfaithful angels, demons and pre-Adamites in the Antechaotic age, and which broke out anew with Adam in the Antediluvian age. All human rebels will be resurrected to face judgment and be confined to eternal hell with all other rebels. Righteous Angels and men will serve God and help Him administer the affairs of the universe forever.

7. **God's Provision for Redemption**: God's provision of Salvation through Christ is eternal for those who accept and conform to it during their probation on earth.

The resurrected Saints who are to reign as Kings and priests with Christ for 1000 years will have been saved from all sin and possibility of rebellion by this time.

The natural people who remain true to God in the last rebellion on earth will be saved to enter the Eternal Kingdom – to multiply and replenish the earth eternally as God originally planned when man was created. The full benefit of redemption will then be realized and enjoyed eternally.

The earth by then would had gone through 3 perfect states and 2 sinful careers.

9. DISPENSATION OF FAITHFULL ANGELS AND THE REDEEMED.

Eternity. World Without End.

So called because Faithful Angels and Resurrected Saints will help God administer the affairs of the universe from the earth which will be the eternal headquarters of His government.

This dispensation is what we know as The New Heaven and the New Earth. It could also be called the Eternal Future, the Eternal Perfect State or the Eternal Sinless Career of the Earth, for it is to be an age of eternal ages, like an endless chain with endless links.

1. **Length**: Eternity, world Without End. It will be the time of perpetual generations, endless perfection and eternal life.
2. **Beginning**: Not only in the beginning but continuing throughout eternity. There will be perfect conditions and people.
3. **Test**: There will be no further need of moral or probationary tests to see if angels or men will prove true and worthy of eternal trust. All in the eternal ruling class – the elect and faithful among angels and men will have been purged of all possibility of falling. They will be obedient to God, and will be absolutely and eternally trusted by God to help administer the affairs of the vast creations. Perpetual generations to come, who will be ruled by resurrected saints and others will be born sinless.
4. **Purpose of God in Testing and Means Used**: To be All-in-All again as before rebellion began with Lucifer and Adam and to carry out God's eternal plan of having

creations and kingdoms which are willingly subject to Him and consecrated to the same end that He is consecrated to; THE HIGHEST GOOD OF BEING FOR ALL.

That is the purpose of God in the future eternal dispensation.

He will continue to use Christ, faithful angels, and redeemed men who will have proved themselves trustworthy as means in ministering to the human race. They would have come with Christ to take over the Kingdoms of this world.

5. **Failure:** there will be no failure throughout eternity with elect angels, elect resurrected men or elect natural men who will carry out their parts of the program as in the eternal purpose of God as His plan was before Adam's fall.

The fall did not do away with God's plan; it only postponed it until the restitution of all things in the New Earth.

6. **Judgment:** there will be no judgment for sin again, for all will be righteous and holy. There will be no more curse.
7. **God's Provision of Redemption**: Same as in previous dispositions – The redemption provided through Christ at the cross is eternal in its scope and benefits to mankind.

To Think Correctly and Accurately is To Know The Truth.

Knowing the Truth Will Set You Free.

CHAPTER THIRTEEN

CONCLUSION

All things are thought process. Man has accomplished the seemingly impossible because he has refused to consider it impossible. By concentration, man have made the connection between the finite and infinite, between the limited and the unlimited, the visible and the invisible, the personal and the impersonal.

Our Actions governed by our Intention, are the products of our Thoughts. Our Thoughts are the components of our Heredity, Environment, Association and Knowledge we have acquired. Hence the dominating thought of a man determines who he is.

Deep feeling gives vitality to thought. Then the will, which is the earnest desire, holds it steady until the "Law of Growth" brings it into manifestation.

The Feeling ---- The Thought----- The Will ---- The Action ------ The Manifestation which ultimately is the reality.

Life is exchange of service. You give and then receive. In Nature giving comes before receiving, but we sometimes get it wrong when we think that we have to receive before we can give. In fact we receive to the measure of what we give.

The athlete may read books and lessons on physical training all his life, but unless he begins to give out strength by actual work, he will never receive any strength; he will eventually get exactly what he gives, but he will have to give it first.

It is exactly the same with us. We will get exactly what we give, but we shall have to give it first. It will then return to us many folds.

Therefore in giving thoughts of Courage, Inspiration, Health or help of any kind, we are setting causes in motion which will bring about their effects.

The quantity received depends not only on the amount given out, but also on the quality of what is given out. That is why skilled workers are remunerated higher than unskilled workers for the same hours of services given.

Knowledge enhances the quality of service we are able to give. You can only give what you have. That is why we need to acquire knowledge. My people perish for lack of knowledge is a scientific truth.

Knowledge when acquired needs to be used and express as service. This is when it is of benefit to mankind. Knowledge acquired but unused becomes ATROPHY. This is what happens when a sick person that stayed too long on the sick bed needs to learn how to walk again.

Knowledge is power and is contingent upon a proper use of the power already in our possession. Unless we give out what we have, the channel where we receive will be obstructed and we receive no more. A cup full of water is unable to accommodate further liquid until there is outflow and some dispensed.

We cannot obtain what we lack if we tenaciously cling to what we have. YOU HAVE TO GIVE FOR

YOU TO GET.

The energy in us utilizes cells of our body when we think, same as when we use these cell when we physically performs functions. These cells are created new by the process of converting food, water and air into the living tissue.

Every action of the brain and every movement of the muscle mean destruction and consequent death of some of these cells. The accumulation of these dead, unused and wasted cells is what causes pain, suffering and disease.

When we allow such destructive thoughts as fear, anger, worry, hatred and jealousy to take possession and these thoughts influence the various functional activities of the body, the brain, the nerves, the heart, the liver or the kidneys. They in turn refuse to perform their various functions; the constructive process cease and destructive process begins.

It is therefore of primary important to imbibe methods whereby we can substitute acts of constructive thinking to those found to produce destructive and unbearable effects.

Mind is a system of vibration. The brain is a vibrator. Thought is the organized effect of each particular vibration when expressed through the requisite combination of cells.

It is not the number of cells, but their vibratory adaptability that gives range to the thoughts of which the mind is capable.

It is through the Universal Mind that the seeds of thought enter the brains of man, so that it conceives thought, which becomes a current of energy,

Centripetal in the mind of man, and Centrifugal in the Universal Mind – Infinite Intelligent.

These seeds of thought have a tendency to germinate to sprout and to grow. They thus form what we call ideas.

When a mental picture is formed in the brain, the rate of vibration corresponding to that picture is immediately awakened in the ether. It depends, however, upon whether the will or desire principle is acting as to whether that vibration mares inward or outward.

If the will is used, the vibration moves outward and the principle of force is put into operation. If the desire nature is awakened, the vibration moves inward, and the law of attraction is put into operation.

In either case, the law of causation expresses itself through the embodying or creative principle.

When we sin, we sin because we choose to. We cannot blame Fate, Kismet, Predestination or God. The Scripture says 'When tempted, no one should say, am tempted of God' For God cannot be tempted by evil, nor does He tempt anyone; but each one is tempted when, by his own evil desire , he is dragged away and enticed.

Interestingly, many people who choose to sin are annoyed by the negative consequences of their sin. "A man's own folly ruins his life; yet his heart rages against the LORD" This is very insightful. When a man foolishly wrecks his life, he may yet insist on blaming God or the devil or perhaps fate. Remorseless eludes him and he persists in his folly.

Man was created with the ability to make moral choices and that he is responsible for those choices.

THINK OUT YOUR DESTINY

The Fall of Man was not a predetermined event in which Adam and Eve were hapless victims of a Puppet-Master God. On the contrary, Adam and his wife had the ability to choose obedience (with its attendant blessing) or disobedience (With its consequent curse). They knew what the result of their decision would be, and they were held accountable.

Being held accountable for choices continued in " You reap what you sow", and also extended to "All hard work brings profit ; but mere talk leads only to poverty. They are all consequences of our actions. Principle of cause and effect.

The decisions we make and circumstances that come our ways, many times in our lives, dropped us, crumpled us, and ground us into the dirt. We feel as though we are worthless.

But whatever happened or about to happen; you are still priceless to those who love you. The worth of our lives come by who we are not in what we do or who we know.

We are each very special to those who love us. So count your blessings not your problems.

Amateurs built the Ark which never sank; professionals built the Titanic but it sank. If God brings you to it, He will bring you through it.

Lest we get the wrong idea, we are not the sovereign master of our fate. Only God is Sovereign. His Sovereign Control is called "providence".

God has chosen to give us a free will, and He has created a moral universe in which the law of cause and effect is a reality. But God is God alone, and there is no accident in the Universe. The Providence of God is working to bring about His plan for creation.

What God announces, He does, although He may have announced it centuries ahead of time. It is therefore pointless to work against the plan of God. There is no wisdom, no insight, no plan that can succeed against the Lord. Even what we would normally call chance or fate is under God's control.

Everything that happens in the world is made to work out according to God's purpose. Evil exists, but it is not allowed to thwart God' providence. God uses even sinful men for His purposes. For the heart of the King, is in His hand; He directs it like a watercourse wherever He pleases.

Men's intent when they crucified Jesus was purely evil, but God allowed it because it brings about His will. God uses the ridiculous to bring about the miraculous.

God's plan includes a reward for those who trust in Him, and He promises to glorify His children. As it is written "No eye has seen, no ear has heard, no mind has conceived what God has prepared for those who love Him".

God gave us freedom to choose our course of actions; but exercising that freedom against God's plan can be painful and chaotic. Whereas exercising our freedom to follow God's plan brings blessings.

God blesses the obedient, He gives those that disobey chance to repent, and consequence for disobedient without remorse and repentance. Sinners shall not go unpunished.

God has a plan for our lives, which include our joy and His Glory both in this world and in the world to come. Those who accept Christ as Savior have accepted God's plan. From then on, it's a step by step following of God's best for us, praying for His will to be done and avoiding the side-track of sin.

God's eternal plan cannot change and is still on course. He continues His plan to be All-in-All, having creations and kingdoms which are willingly subjected to Him and consecrated to the same end that He Himself is consecrated to; THE HIGHEST GOOD OF BEING FOR ALL.

He will continue to use Christ, Faithful Angels, and Redeemed men who will have proved themselves trustworthy as means in ministering to the human race.

The Principle of Attraction is expressed in Love. It governs the seemingly involuntary affinities of minerals and vegetable substances, passions of animals and the love of men.

The Law of Love is a piece of pure science, and the oldest and simplest form of love is the elective affinity of two differing cells.

Above all laws is the law of love, for love is live.

THE BOOK OF LIVE IS FOUND TO BE A LOVE STORY.

TO GOD BE THE GLORY.

Books Published by JESUS FRIENDS MINISTRY

AFFLICTION – Fruit of Sin explained what constitute acceptable and perfect will of God. Do not be a slumber but be wise and claim your inheritance which the devil had usurped from you. The book also explained what redemption stands for, the powerlessness of the devil and how to use the key that Christians possess which open the door of life. We have been bought with a price. It is therefore non-excusable for us Christians not to be remorse and resolve to ease doing wrong and start to do what is right. Various Doctrines as explained in this book testifies to the mysteries and serve as the lifeboat to rescue believers from the storm of life. **"The Redeemed Man"** is a lifeboat to rescue and bring brethren to shore of salvation.

Contact Us @;

12, Pecham Park Road, London. SE15 6TW

E—mail kaenis1@yahoo.co.uk

Tel: 07427942000, 07951775255

Kayode Eniraiyetan

Born Poor: Die Rich teaches the true philosophy upon which personal success is all about. Every great achievement began in the imagination of one person. Wherever you are, whoever you are, whatever your calling, there is chance for you to make yourself useful and productive by developing and using your imagination. The three things which all mankind desires and which are necessary for his highest expression and complete development are **Health, Wealth and Love**. Hence those who possess all three find nothing else which can be added to their happiness.

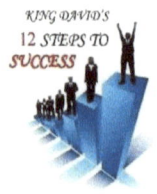

We all have dreams, wishes and aspirations, but to attain such, we must overcome some obstacles, some challenges and stumbling blocks. These are our life's "Battle of Goliath". They are the great physical or spiritual hardships we must bear and once we overcome them, we get the ladder that takes us to the mountain top from the valley of life. The book: **KING DAVID'S 12 STEPS TO SUCCESS** are those battle gears, the arsenal we need for our victorious end and the success we all envisage in our dreams and aspirations.

The moment a person becomes a born again Christian, he/she becomes the target for the devil. **The 7 Solid Walls Protecting A Christian** are the Spiritual Bodyguards God automatically appointed to every child of God at the moment they become born again. They are invincible. They have limitless power and their services had been paid fully through the blood of Jesus. They are the angels God assigned to protect us to ensure no harm befalls us.

ABOUT THE AUTHOR

Kayode Eniraiyetan is an Associate of the Chartered Institute of Bankers (ACIB) of both England and Nigeria.

He has a Master of Science in Banking and Finance from University of Benin, Nigeria, and his banking career spanned over twenty-five years in which ten was as Branch Manager in various banking institutions in Nigeria.

Kayode Eniraiyetan is the Founder and Coordinator of **JESUS' FRIENDS MINISTRY** (a Ministry that share the Scripture Knowledge through publications). He has been a worker in the Lord's vineyard for over thirty years.

He is the Senior Partner **KAENIS CONSULT LTD, a** Finance Consulting firm. He lives in London.

www.ingramcontent.com/pod-product-compliance
Lightning Source LLC
Chambersburg PA
CBHW042309150426
43198CB00001B/11